# COUNTRY INSIGHTS
# BRAZIL

## Marion Morrison

WAYLAND

# COUNTRY INSIGHTS

## BRAZIL • CHINA • FRANCE • JAMAICA • JAPAN • KENYA • MEXICO • PAKISTAN

## GUIDE TO THIS BOOK

As well as telling you about the whole of Brazil, this book looks closely at the city of São Paulo and the village of Horto.

 This city symbol will appear at the top of the page and information boxes each time São Paulo is looked at.

 This rural symbol will appear each time Horto is looked at.

**Cover photograph:** Children from the city of Rio de Janeiro.

**Title page:** The Rio de Janeiro Carnival takes place every year in February or March. Sixteen samba schools take part, each with up to 5,000 dancers.

**Contents page:** Houses in the north-east of Brazil are built simply from wattle and daub, and covered with plaster.

Series and book editor: Polly Goodman
Series and book designer: Tim Mayer
Production Controller: Caroline Davis
Consultant: Dr. Tony Binns, Geography lecturer and tutor of student teachers at the University of Sussex.

First published in 1996 by
Wayland Publishers Ltd
61 Western Road, Hove
East Sussex, BN3 1JD, England

**British Library Cataloguing in Publication Data**
Morrison, Marion
    Brazil. – (Country Insights)
    1. Brazil – Juvenile literature
    I. Title
    981'.064

ISBN 0 7502 2013 9

Typeset by Tim Mayer, England
Printed and bound in Italy by LEGO S.p.A., Vicenza.

# Contents

# Introducing Brazil

Brazil covers about half the continent of South America and is the fifth-largest country in the world. It shares borders with ten countries, and the Brazilian coast along the Atlantic Ocean is one of the longest of any country in the world. Brazil extends from north of the equator southwards to beyond the Tropic of Capricorn. Almost half of the country is part of the Amazon basin, a low area of land that is drained by the world's biggest river, the Amazon. Brazil's highest mountain, Pico da Neblina, is 3,014 metres high and lies in the far north. The largest lake, Patos, is in the south-east.

In April 1500, the Portuguese explorer Pedro Álvares Cabral was the first European to reach Brazil. Cabral named the country Vera Cruz, or 'Land of the True Cross'. Soon after, the country became known as Brazil, after the valuable Brazil-wood found in the forests along the coast. The land was inhabited by groups of native American Indians.

*The famous beach of Copacabana, in Rio de Janeiro.*

**▲ This book will take you to the city of São Paulo and the village of Horto, as well as the rest of Brazil. You can find these places on the map.**

| BRAZIL | |
|---|---|
| **Population:** | **162 million. Brazil has the sixth-largest population in the world.** |
| **Area:** | **8,512 km²** |
| **States:** | **Twenty-six states and one Federal District.** |
| **Time zones:** | **Brazil is so vast that there are four time zones across the width of the country and its offshore islands.** |
| **Language:** | **Portuguese** |

The Portuguese settled in the coastal region, and later brought slaves from Africa to work on the sugar plantations. During the nineteenth and twentieth centuries, other nationalities, including Italians, Japanese and Germans settled in Brazil.

Brazil was a Portuguese colony for about 300 years. From 1807 it was ruled by members of the Portuguese royal family until, in 1889, it became a republic with a president. Today the president lives in Brasilia, the new capital city, which was founded in 1960.

# The city of São Paulo

▲ *Concrete tower blocks range from the centre of São Paulo for as far as the eye can see.*

São Paulo, which means Saint Paul, is the largest, most wealthy city in Brazil. It is also the largest city in South America and the third largest in the world. São Paulo lies in the south-east, in a highland region that was once covered by forest. The city is less than 75 kilometres from the coast.

São Paulo was founded in 1554 by two priests. In the seventeenth century, early pioneers, known as *bandeirantes*, used the city as a base, from which they set out to explore west into the interior of Brazil. Only 100 years ago, São Paulo was still a small town with about 30,000 people and mainly mud-brick buildings. At the beginning of the twentieth century, thousands of immigrants began to arrive from Europe and Japan. They cultivated the land, grew coffee and invested in businesses.

◄ *Office workers in the city centre wait for their bus home.*

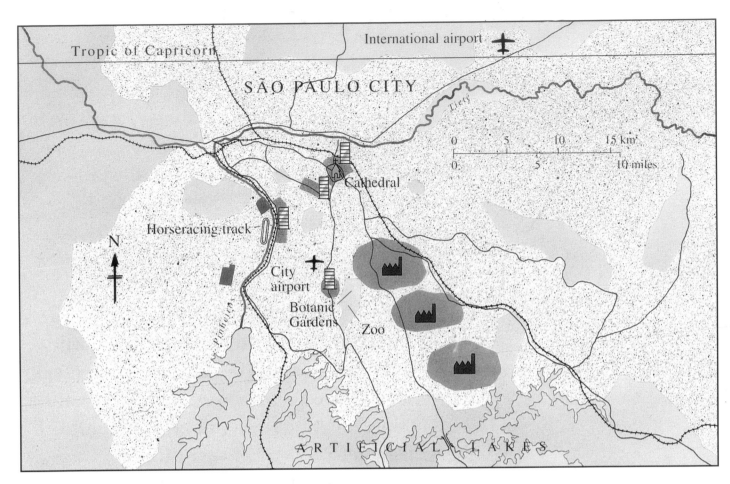

By the 1930s, São Paulo's main street was bordered by fine houses of the wealthy. By the 1960s, high-rise offices and apartments had begun to appear in the city centre. Today, the city has several centres and many suburbs. Most old buildings have now been replaced by huge concrete tower blocks.

The people of São Paulo are known as *paulistanos*, and they are noted for their hard-working nature. Not all *paulistanos* are wealthy, however, and many live in areas of simple housing known as *favelas*.

### KEY TO MAP

| | |
|---|---|
| —— | Major roads |
| +++ | Railway/Metro |
|  | Banking and highrise, central business zone. |
|  | Industrial areas |
|  | Shopping centres |
|  | Parkland |
| | Built-up areas, including business and residential. |

### SÃO PAULO'S POPULATION

| | |
|---|---|
| Inner city: | 9.4 million |
| Greater city (including suburbs and *favelas*): | 17 million |

# The village of Horto

▲ *Villagers chat in the main street of Horto.*

Horto is a small village of tiled houses in the state of Ceará, in north-east Brazil. The north-east is Brazil's poorest region. Droughts are frequent and can last many months. One drought, in 1877, was so bad that tens of thousands of people died. Yet 30 per cent of Brazil's population lives in this region and it is the second most densely populated region in Brazil after the south-east. The difference is that in the north-east, one-in-four people live in rural areas such as Horto, compared with only one-in-ten in the south-east.

▶ *This family uses their donkey to get to the market.*

In Horto, there is a church and a main square, a small medical store, a general store and several schools. The village is connected to the town of Juazeiro do Norte, 12 kilometres away, by three roads. The shortest roads are dusty and unpaved. These roads cross a small river by a simple bridge. The other road is longer and paved. The land between the town and village is dotted with palm trees and there are small farms with sugarcane plantations. The people of Horto are mainly descendants of mixed marriages between the Portuguese settlers and the original native American people.

| HORTO'S POPULATION | |
| --- | --- |
| Horto village: | 1,219 |

KEY TO MAP

 Houses

Scrub forest

Farmland and sugar plantations

Tarmac road

Dirt road

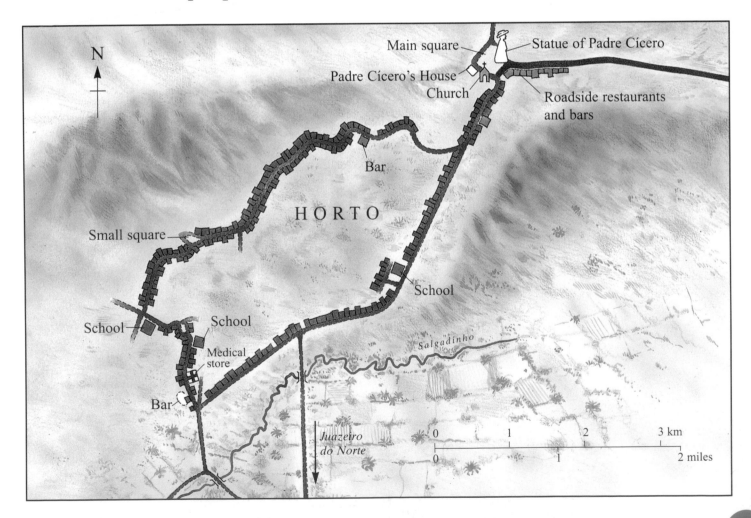

# Land and climate

The Amazon river drains much of northern Brazil, with tributaries entering the river from many of the surrounding countries. One-third of Brazil is covered by the Amazon rain forest, the world's largest rain forest. Some of the land is so low that it is flooded for much of the year. Elsewhere, much of the land in Brazil is based on some of the oldest rocks in the world. Over millions of years, these rocks have been worn away leaving valleys, canyons, steep-sided hills and large expanses of flat highlands, known to Brazilians as the *planaltos*. In the north are the Guiana highlands, while the Brazilian highlands cover the centre of the country. Along the coast is a range of hills called the Great Escarpment. Most of Brazil, however, is less than 900 metres above sea-level. The Amazon basin has heavy rainfall and has temperatures of 25–30 °C throughout the year. In the south, the climate is cooler and it sometimes snows in the winter.

◀ **Canoes are the usual transport along the many Amazon rivers.**

## BRAZIL'S LAND AND CLIMATE

The Amazon river is the second-longest in the world, after the Nile, in Egypt. It has the largest volume of water of any river, and the force of the water leaving the mouth of the Amazon is so great that there is fresh water 160 kilometres off the coast.

The length of Brazil's Atlantic coast is 7,408 kilometres.

The River São Francisco is known as Brazil's national river because it is the only large river that begins and ends in Brazil. It is 2,900 kilometres long.

▲ A farmworker leads his horse and its foal in the dry, north-east of Brazil.

▲ A rainbow falls over the Iguazu Falls, on the border with Argentina.

Brazil is rich in mineral resources, including lead, gold, platinum, copper, bauxite and manganese. One of world's largest deposits of iron ore has been discovered in the Amazon region, and the country is the world's largest producer of coffee and sugar. Coal, gas and oil deposits help to supply energy, which also comes from hydroelectricity from dams on some of the country's great rivers. These include the River São Francisco in the north-east and the River Parana in the south. The Iguazu Falls is a tributary of the Parana river and is a major tourist attraction. It consists of 275 waterfalls over a precipice almost 3 kilometres wide.

# São Paulo's land and climate

*Looking over the Tieté river at the city. If you were to stand at this spot, you would smell the pollution in the river from industrial and household waste.*

The city of São Paulo lies on the southern edge of the Brazilian highlands in the south of Brazil. From one side of the city, steep valleys lead down through dense forest to swamps, and the Atlantic coast. On the other three sides, the city is surrounded by low hills with valleys, through which the highly polluted Tieté river passes on its way across the highlands. Later, the Tieté joins the Parana river which supplies the Itaipú hydroelectric dam. This dam is the second-largest source of hydroelectric power in the world and most of its electricity is used by São Paulo city.

Close to the city there are many small towns and over 30,000 factory sites. Beyond the city, the reddish-coloured tropical earth is good for

| SÃO PAULO'S LAND AND CLIMATE | |
|---|---|
| Height: | 760 metres above sea-level |
| Average rainfall: | 1,194 mm a year. |
| Temperature: | Minimum:  3°C |
| | Maximum:  28°C |

agriculture and cattle ranching. Coffee has been the most successful crop on this land, but today oranges, rice, cotton and soya are also grown. The state of São Paulo covers less than 3 per cent of the country, but it produces about 20 per cent of Brazil's agricultural output and over 60 per cent of its industrial goods. Most of the imports and exports of the state pass through Santos, the closest port to the city.

São Paulo city stands on the Tropic of Capricorn, but the high altitude means that the climate does not always feel tropical. The warmest months are from November to March, which is summer in the southern hemisphere. The coldest time is usually in June or July, when it can be frosty, especially outside the city. A rainy season begins in the summer, often bringing flooding and landslides.

▲ *Coffee pickers and their truck on a plantation near the city. Coffee is Brazil's major crop. It is grown on plantations like this one, all over the south-east of Brazil.*

◄ *Cowboys round up cattle on a ranch to the west of the city. Cattle ranching is a major business in São Paulo state.*

13

# Horto's land and climate

The village of Horto was built on the side of a low range of hills. Much of the vegetation surrounding the village is a thorny forest of trees and bushes.

**The farmers of the backlands are hardy people who live in a tough, dry climate.**

Low hills, or *serras*, stand above flat plains. Some hills are bare, while others that catch more rain are well forested.

The villagers of Horto depend on agriculture and the extraction of minerals from the earth to make money. Farms grow sugar-cane and fruit such as bananas, mangoes and avocado pears. Cattle are raised in the backlands, and their skins are used for a variety of leather products. Copper ore is found nearby. There are also valuable deposits of granite, a fine asbestos for industrial use and clay for pottery found locally.

Rainfall in the village is heaviest in March and April. In July and August there is almost no rain. The strong sun and dry winds evaporate much of the water and irrigation is essential to grow crops. Water for the village comes from special wells bored in the valley. Since Horto is near the equator, there is little change in temperature throughout the year, although at night the air is cooler. It is never frosty and most days begin with warm sun.

*The backlands of the north-east are covered with thorny forests, studded with cactus plants.*

## HORTO'S LAND AND CLIMATE

| | |
|---|---|
| Height: | 605 metres above sea-level. |
| Average rainfall: | 950 mm a year. |
| Temperature: | Minimum: 23 °C |
| | Maximum: 33 °C |

# Home life

Family life is important to Brazilians. In poorer, rural communities, several generations often live together under one roof. Grandparents help look after the children while the parents go to work. In the cities, families are usually smaller, but they get together frequently. Children from poorer homes sometimes have to work to help the family survive.

Brazilian homes vary greatly. Some of the simplest homes belong to the peoples of the Amazon rain forest. These homes are made from wood and palm thatch collected from the forest. Situated near rivers, they are often built on stilts to protect them from flooding. Shanty towns, or *favelas*, around the cities are made of brick, or plywood, with corrugated-iron roofs. In contrast, lavish mansions and luxury apartments are found in many Brazilian cities.

**A family from north-east Brazil.**

There are also single-storey homes with gardens, and grand but decaying houses from Portuguese colonial days. In the south, some immigrant German communities have kept the style of their original homes in Bavaria.

There is a great variety of food in Brazil. In the Amazon, river fish is popular. Around Salvador, African-style dishes are made with seafood, rich palm oil and coconut milk. In the cattle country of the south, meat is served at every meal. Perhaps the most typical Brazilian food is black beans and rice, served with manioc flour, or *farofa*, and a spicy sauce. Sometimes meat, fish, chicken or sausages are added. Street markets throughout Brazil sell all kinds of fruit.

A Bahian woman from Salvador, on the east coast, sells African-style foods. Many people in this region are descended from slaves brought from Africa to work on the sugar plantations.

## TWO FAVOURITE BRAZILIAN DISHES

*Feijoada Completa* This dish is usually served as lunch on Saturdays. It is a black-bean and meat stew, with smoked ham and spicy sausages. It is eaten with rice, fried pork, boiled kale, *farofa* and slices of fresh orange.

*Moqueca* An African-Brazilian dish of fish, including shrimps and shellfish, cooked with palm oil, grated coconut and spices. It is eaten with rice that is cooked in coconut milk.

# Home life in São Paulo

In São Paulo, many people live in tall apartment blocks. Senhor and Senhora Campos live with their three children on the eleventh floor of a luxurious apartment block, with its own swimming pool and garden. Their apartment has a living room, a separate dining room, bathroom, a kitchen and a room where clothes are washed. There is also a room and toilet for a maid, who lives with the family and is paid to help Senhora Campos with the cooking and cleaning. The Campos' have friends who live in the suburbs, with large houses in tree-lined avenues. Even in poorer suburbs,

**'I travel an hour by bus to get to work at seven in the morning.'
– Fatima Andrade, maid.**

**TELEVISION OWNERSHIP IN SÃO PAULO**

In an average suburb, 100 per cent of households have one or more televisions. Even in the *favelas*, the majority of families have a television.

*Life for thousands of people in São Paulo means a **favela** home such as these.*

◄ *Wealthy families in São Paulo have homes with tennis courts, often surrounded by woodland.*

most houses have water and electricity, although food is often cooked with gas. There is piped gas in some parts of the city, but many people use gas-filled cylinders, which can be refilled when they are empty.

Home life for people in the *favelas* is much more difficult. The Soares family have no water, electric light or toilets. They live and do their cooking in just one room, although they do have a television. A low-cost housing project of simple apartment blocks has been started to help families like the Soares. The blocks are built with stairs and no lifts to avoid expensive maintenance costs.

People in São Paulo buy their food in small shops, supermarkets and from street markets. For lunch, Senhor Campos eats in a restaurant in the city centre. But his assistant, Milton Rodrigues, usually buys a snack from a fast-food bar, or a stall in the street. The evening meal is a time when families get together. They often eat at home, but many people also enjoy eating out in local restaurants.

▲ *The wealthy of São Paulo shop in elaborate shopping centres like this one, El Dorado Shopping Centre.*

# Home life in Horto

*A boy with his family's donkeys, outside their house. The house is made from wattle and mud bricks.*

Many houses in Horto are built with walls of wattle and daub, a mixture of sticks and mud that is covered with plaster when dry. Homes usually have three or four small rooms and most have electricity. The Coelho family live in a house with wooden doors split in two, so the lower half can be kept shut to keep their animals in or out. Their back yard is fenced in by spiny bushes to keep the animals in. The Coelho family has chickens, but other families have a pig, or a donkey which they use for work. Cages of tiny birds hang in the shade on the outside walls of many homes. A few modern homes have been built on the outskirts of the village, but *favelas* do not exist in Horto since even the poorest people can build solid homes using local materials.

Almost everyone in the village knows everybody else. Most houses face directly on to the street and doors are left open so that neighbours can call in for a chat. Families are very important in Horto. Everyone in the Coelho family eats and watches television in the same room, and any friends and neighbours without a television are always welcome to join them.

**TELEVISION OWNERSHIP IN HORTO**

Out of every ten families, about seven have a television.

20

The village has no large shops, supermarkets or restaurants, but there are several small bars where Senhor Coelho and his friends gather to talk or have a drink. For most people, a main meal is rice and beans with meat. A few families have refrigerators, but otherwise meat is usually salted and dried in the sun. This is called *carne-de-sol*, or sun meat.

'My sister and I often have to carry buckets of water home.' – Ana Maria Coelho, aged 12.

Horto is often so dry that water has to be collected from a standpipe and carried home.

# Brazil at work

Some Brazilian men and women work in professions as doctors, dentists or nurses, or as lawyers, scientists or teachers. Others work in factories, in car-assembly plants and in shipbuilding, especially around São Paulo. Brazil's merchant ships provide work for sailors, and there are also many river boats, especially on the Amazon river. Other people are employed in transport, as bus or taxi drivers. There are also pilots and cabin staff in Brazil's three major international and many regional airline services. Since new schools, hospitals, homes and roads are needed all the time, the construction industry provides work for engineers and labourers all over the country. In the south, many men and women work on large-scale farms, in coffee plantations or on cattle ranches.

*Harvesting maize on a large farm.*

During the last thirty years, people have moved into the Amazon region from other parts of the country, looking for work and a better life. For people with smallholdings and animals, this has often been unsuccessful. But work in the towns and cities of the Amazon region is much the same as elsewhere, with shops, offices, industries and computers. In parts of the Amazon, large mines have been developed, which employ people of many different skills. Some of the mining centres are small towns, with many different facilities, from hospitals to schools, banks and cinemas.

▲ *The timber industry of the Amazon area supplies international markets with valuable hardwoods, such as mahogany.*

| TYPE OF WORK IN BRAZIL | |
| --- | --- |
| | Percentage of population |
| Agriculture | 28 |
| Manufacturing | 25 |
| Services | 47 |

◀ *Rubbish is cleared by settlers, before they claim the land.*

# Work in São Paulo

**The crowded pavements of São Paulo's business centre.**

São Paulo is the commercial and business centre of Brazil and many people work in banks and offices. They control the money made from exports, insurance and investments of all kinds. People who work in these companies are usually skilled in using computers and speak several languages. Some travel on business all over the world, while others travel just across Brazil. In the factories around the city, many household goods are made, such as televisions and washing machines. Other products include clothing, paper, and plastics. Many of Brazil's leading magazine and book publishers are based in São Paulo, giving work to editors, photographers and printers.

The Cunha family is a typically prosperous family in the city. Senhor Cunha works for a travel company, while Senhora Cunha runs a small shop. Their two eldest children, Maria do Carno and Antonio, have finished college and are now training in industry and management. Maria is a secretary and Antonio is an interpreter. Poorer families than the Cunhas often work as bus and taxi drivers, shop assistants and restaurant staff, receptionists and cleaners, flower sellers and street traders. People without jobs in the city make a living as best they can by doing odd

'Most days I do three jobs. A friend and I share a taxi and I drive it in the mornings. Then I do house repairs in the afternoon and work in a bar at night.' – Mauricio Arauyo, taxi driver.

jobs or selling trinkets from street stalls. Many children from the *favelas*, like Geraldo and Juliano, work in the streets cleaning shoes or washing cars.

People in São Paulo travel to work using public transport, private cars, taxis and even helicopters. The metro and buses are affordable for most people. During rush hours, traffic is often brought to a standstill because there are so many cars.

▲ *A car-assembly plant on the outskirts of São Paulo.*

◄ *Newspapers are sold on the streets in all the Brazilian cities. Many cities publish their own newspapers.*

# Work in Horto

*A family of basket makers outside their home.*

It is not easy to find work in villages like Horto. Some people go to Juazeiro do Norte to work in offices, shops or restaurants. At harvest time, others get jobs as cutters on sugar-cane plantations up to 20 kilometres from the village. But in the village itself, people work on the land growing fruit or vegetables for the market. They make goods such as basketware and items of wood furniture which they sell. A few people, like Senhor and Senhora Pereira and Joao Barbosa, own small shops or bars, and housebuilding is shared amongst the men. The village is kept clean by the villagers, who regularly sweep the road and pavement in front of their houses.

Horto is luckier than many villages, because its history provides an unusual source of work. Three times a year, thousands of visitors arrive to visit the statue and grave of Padre Cícero, a local priest who lived over 100 years ago. Cícero's house is near the village square. It is believed that the spirit of the priest can cure people who visit his grave and almost 2 million pilgrims visit Horto every year. The pilgrimages provide temporary work for many

26

people. The streets have to be cleaned, the markets are busy, children sell religious candles and act as porters. Candles are made during the rest of the year and thousands of miniature statues of Padre Cícero are produced from plaster of Paris. A small factory makes jewellery and religious pendants, which are sold by street traders as souvenirs to the pilgrims.

▲ Cutting sugar-cane on a plantation near Horto village. Sugar-cane was one of the first crops introduced into the north-east of Brazil by Portuguese settlers.

'Once the children have gone to school, I spend many hours making souvenirs for the pilgrims.' – Maria Joselino, housewife, Horto.

◄ Maria Joselino makes these plaster-cast miniature statues of Padre Cícero every year and dries them in the sun.

# Going to school

All Brazilian children between the ages of seven and fourteen must go to school in Brazil. Sometimes this is difficult for children of rural families, who have to help their parents work on the land, or for the children from *favelas* who have to work on the streets. But schooling is now available for most Brazilians, even for people of the Amazon rain forests. In the past, the only education Amazon children had was from missionaries, but there are now sixty teaching centres for the Amazon peoples. Lessons also reach remote parts of Brazil by television and radio.

*A group of secondary-school students from the city of Salvador, in north-east Brazil.*

Schools are run either by the state or the church, or are paid for privately. There are many more schools in the cities than in rural areas.

Children from wealthier families can start school when they are very young, at a play group or infant school. There are about 30 million school-age students in Brazil and the country's young population is increasing rapidly, so Brazil needs many schools. New schools are often built to the same design as older schools so they can be built quickly. They have young teachers who start work straight from college.

University or college is available for students, without charge, provided they get high enough exam grades. Most students attend the university nearest their home, or stay with relatives, to save money. But university is still too expensive for many students. School leavers from poorer families often go directly to jobs. Private language schools in the cities, which teach English or other European languages, are very popular amongst wealthier students.

▲ *A game of volleyball in a secondary school in the Amazon region.*

▲ *Many young children work on the city streets to earn money. These two boys are carrying their shoe-cleaning equipment.*

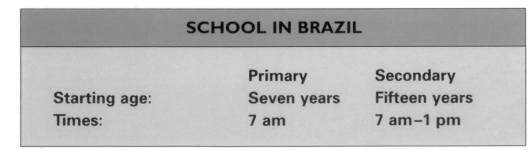

| SCHOOL IN BRAZIL | | |
|---|---|---|
| | Primary | Secondary |
| Starting age: | Seven years | Fifteen years |
| Times: | 7 am | 7 am–1 pm |

# School in São Paulo

São Paulo has grown so quickly over the last thirty years that many new schools have been built. Those in the wealthier districts are bigger and better equipped. For example, students in the wealthier schools learn how to use computers, but poorer schools cannot afford the machines. Most children in the city attend school. The unlucky ones are the children who live or work on the streets. Over 90 per cent of children over fourteen years old in São Paulo can read, write and count.

**'My father has no job so he can help me with my homework.' – Auta da Silva, 7 years old, from a *favela* in São Paulo.**

Pupils of all schools in the city wear a simple uniform. Girls usually wear white blouses and dark-coloured skirts, while boys wear white shirts and dark trousers. Boys and girls wear a badge on their tops which identifies their school. Children walk, cycle or travel by bus to school, although a few are taken by car.

School starts and finishes early to avoid the afternoon heat. Most schools start at 7 am and finish soon after lunch, at 1 pm. If there is a shortage of classrooms, schools 'double up', meaning they take young pupils in the morning and older students in the afternoon. One of the advantages of living in São Paulo is that students can visit museums and galleries. Lessons also include sports. Football, called *futebol*, is the most popular sport at school. Almost every school can find a patch of ground where pupils can play. Other sports include basketball and volleyball, and in wealthier schools there are often tennis courts and a swimming pool.

*Teenage college students in São Paulo taking a lunch break.*

31

# School in Horto

Horto has three schools, two primary and one secondary. All three are run and paid for by the state. There are a total of 800 pupils, which means that over half the people living in Horto are at school. The schools in the village are simple but well attended. Classes begin at 7 am and continue until midday. Lessons include Brazilian and world history, Portuguese and writing, maths and basic sciences. Most children, like those in São Paulo, wear white blouses or shirts, with clean, neatly pressed blue jeans and trainers.

*Pupils from Horto village cycle to their secondary school in Juazeiro do Norte, 12 kilometres away.*

Some older students go to secondary school in Juazeiro do Norte, which means they have to cycle or walk the 12 kilometres there. Students who get good grades are given the chance to graduate to the regional university in Juazeiro do Norte, or to the technical school. Some decide to go to Fortaleza, the state capital. Sports are popular with all the children, particularly football. Juazeiro do Norte is the local centre for sporting competitions, and any up-and-coming stars from Horto soon find their way to the town.

*Schoolboy footballers in the school stadium in Juazeiro do Norte.*

'I walk to school with Mauricio. It takes us half an hour to get here.' – Marcos Sereno, 8 years old, school pupil.

The schools in Horto are small and the children come from homes that are not wealthy, like many in São Paulo. Local education gives most children a good start for a rural way of life. But there is less opportunity for going into further education than in São Paulo, and more children leave school early to look for work. Fewer people in the north-east of Brazil can read or write than those in the south-east.

# Brazil at play

Brazilians are crazy about football and the nation is world famous for its football teams and stars. Brazil has won the World Football Cup a record four times and it has the world's largest football stadium in Rio de Janeiro, which holds 155,000 people. Other spectator sports include the annual Grand Prix motor racing and horse-racing.

There are facilities for almost every type of sport and leisure pursuit in Brazil, but not everyone can afford them. What everyone can do, if they live on the coast, is go to the beach. In the summer, beaches like Copacabana, in Rio de Janeiro, are packed out. People sunbathe, exercise, jog and play volleyball. They also enjoy watersports. Away from the coast, people relax at weekends by walking, climbing or swimming. They may have a barbecue, or *churrasco*, where there is also dancing, or they may simply watch sport on television.

*People relaxing on a beach near Recife. The sailing boats are based on the design of jangada boats, which are used for fishing on the north-east coast.*

| NATIONAL HOLIDAYS IN BRAZIL | |
| --- | --- |
| 1 Jan | New Year's Day |
| Feb/Mar | Carnival |
| Mar/Apr | Good Friday and Easter Sunday |
| 21 Apr | Tiradentes Day (honours a Brazilian hero) |
| 1 May | Labour Day |
| 18 June | Corpus Christi |
| 7 Sept | Independence Day |
| 12 Oct | Our Lady of Aparecida (patron saint of Brazil) |
| 2 Nov | All Souls Day (Day of the Dead) |
| 15 Nov | Proclamation of the Republic |
| 25 Dec | Christmas Day |

Brazil is also famous for its carnivals, which take place in February or March each year. The Rio Carnival is the most famous and attracts thousands of tourists, but *Carnaval*, as it is known, takes place all over Brazil and everyone likes to take part. Music, dance, spectacular floats and elaborate, colourful costumes are the background to Carnival. Even though it may only last a few days each year, it takes the rest of the year to prepare for. Most Brazilians are traditionally Roman Catholics. But African cults, passed down from when black slaves arrived in Brazil, are becoming increasingly popular. In Rio, the Umbanda followers celebrate the festival to the goddess of the sea, Iemanja, on New Year's Eve.

*Samba dancers on their colourful float in Rio's Carnival.*

# Leisure time in São Paulo

Every weekend during the summer, the highway from São Paulo to the coast is packed with cars. Thousands of people head for the beaches near Santos or along the coast road to Rio de Janeiro. Some of the towns along the way have holiday apartments, weekend chalets and camping sites. Half an hour outside the city is the zoo, which is a favourite place for family outings at the weekends.

Within the city itself there are some excellent facilities for sports. One suburb has a modern stadium that holds 70,000 spectators. It has a floodlit football ground, an athletics field, basketball court, covered gymnasium, open-air and covered tennis courts and a 50-metre-long swimming pool.

*Members of a football team practise in a school sports stadium in São Paulo.*

The city also has a large racecourse for horse-racing, and in recent years the city has hosted an international Grand Prix motor race.

Many *paulistanos* like to relax by going to the ballet or a concert. The city has many theatres, museums, and art galleries, and fashionable nightclubs for young people.

São Paulo's cathedral is in the heart of the city and can hold up to 8,000 worshippers. People in the city attend church regularly. There are an increasing number of new churches being built in the city, for groups such as the Seventh-Day Adventists and The Mormons.

'Working five days a week on the twentieth floor of a bank building, I really look forward to my weekends on the beach.'
– Pedro Oliveira, office worker, São Paolo.

On the beach at Santos, the older men relax with a game of dominoes.

# Leisure time in Horto

Life in Horto is much more relaxed than in São Paulo. At the end of the day, people sit outside their homes in the warm evenings, chatting with friends or sharing a meal and a drink. They play cards or dominoes and sometimes chess. The men may wander off to the local bar where there is a pool table. The women talk about the events of the day or maybe watch television.

'I like to sit with my old friends in the evenings. It is our custom to chat and smoke our pipes.'
– Dona Marta, grandmother, Horto.

*Men from Horto village enjoy a game of cards.*

At weekends, families frequently take a bus or truck to the warm springs and small park at Caldas, about 30 kilometres from the village, where the springs have been converted into swimming pools. In the park, families enjoy picnics at tables under trees, and there is always a chance to play football.

◀ *Warm springs at Caldas, near Horto, have been turned into swimming pools. They make a favourite place for families to visit at the weekends.*

## DANCES IN HORTO

*Forro* is the name given to dance music in the region where Horto is. The music has African and Portuguese origins. Many of the dances are based on folklore. The *Buma-Meu-Boi* dance is the story of a bull that is killed and brought back to life. Music is played on guitars, accordions, flute, drums and an instrument called a *ganzá*.

▲ *Many Horto villagers spend their time off playing a friendly game with dice.*

# The future

Brazilians can look to the twenty-first century with great hope for the future because their country is a huge land with many rich resources. Brazil produces most of what it needs, including oil, and it has a wide range of exports. The population is young, energetic and mostly well-educated. Brazilian engineers work in construction in many parts of the world and many goods produced in Brazil are sold worldwide, including cars and aircraft.

However, as the country's population and industry grows, destruction to the environment increases. The Amazon region has been in the news for a long time. Over 100 years ago, the rain forests supplied most of the world's rubber, and later timber.

*Settlers in the Amazon use the 'slash and burn' method to make clearings, where they can build homes and grow crops.*

Highways were built through the forests and settlers and cattle ranchers moved in. Huge deposits of minerals have now been discovered and hydroelectric dams have been built on some of the tributaries of the Amazon river. All this has threatened the future of the largest area of rain forest left on earth. Scientists worry that too much rain forest has been cleared and Brazilian scientists are also anxious about the damage farming has done to other types of forest in the Amazon region.

The population of Brazil is growing fast, with about 4.5 million extra people every year. This is enough people to fill a city the size of Madrid. Such a large number of people will provide the workforce of the future, and help Brazilian industry. But they also need schools, hospitals and homes. The future for many Brazilians will depend on how well their leaders manage the country's economy.

## BRAZIL'S POPULATION

It is estimated that by the year 2025, Brazil's population will reach 250 million.

In the early sixteenth century, when the Portuguese first arrived, there were between 3–5 million native American Indians. Today there are no more than 20,000 living in scattered communities in the Amazon forest. Not many are likely to survive the twenty-first century.

*Two girls sell fruit and vegetables in the street in Manaus, Brazil's main port on the Amazon river.*

# The future of São Paulo

*A young mother and her children from a favela.*

One of the greatest clouds over the future of São Paulo is pollution. On most days, if you stand on a high building and look across the city, the horizon is lost in a dull brown mist. At times, the air in the city can be so polluted by exhaust fumes that people have streaming eyes and noses. Traffic jams are frequent and the streets are regularly choked with cars. Vehicles are not the only cause of the pollution, however. There are thousands of factories giving off smoke around the city and gas is used in many households.

The Tieté river, which runs through São Paulo to the highlands, is also affected by the pollution of the city. Once clean, it is now an open drain for domestic and industrial rubbish and is so heavily polluted that the authorities have begun a clean-up operation. For example, one riverside area has been turned into a wildlife park. But such schemes have to compete with the rapid growth of the city and its population, which is expected to reach 26 million by the year 2000.

There is no doubt that *paulistanos* want to fight pollution in their city. There is a high standard of education and environmental issues are taught in the schools and universities. Television and magazines in the city have programmes and articles on 'green' issues, and young people are very aware of the problems around them. The future of São Paulo depends on how much is done to stop pollution as the city continues to grow bigger and richer.

## SÃO PAULO'S POPULATION

Of the 9.4 million people living in inner São Paulo, about 20 per cent are of school age and families are smaller than in rural areas. The number of adults is likely to increase as literacy, education and migration from the countryside continues to rise.

▲ Rush-hour traffic is a major cause of pollution in central São Paulo.

◀ Pollution and rubbish in the industrial area of Cubatão, the petrochemical centre for São Paulo.

# The future of Horto

The village of Horto is unlikely to change much in the future since there are no plans for great industrial or agricultural development in the area. The most serious threat to the village is the number of young people likely to leave. Many head for Juazeiro do Norte, Fortaleza, or other cities further away, hoping to find better opportunities than the village can provide. Those who stay behind usually follow their parents and work on the land, or in the small shops. Some will marry and start families, as many rural Brazilians do, when they are still young. The village will survive as long as pilgrims continue to visit the statue and home of Padre Cícero. Not only does this provide work in making candles and mementos, but the pilgrims, however poor, always leave something in the village.

As Juazeiro do Norte expands, Horto may become part of the town, but for now

*Horto overlooks farmland and the dry uplands of Ceará state.*

## HORTO'S POPULATION

Among the 1,219 population of Horto, about 66 per cent are of school age. Families in rural areas marry young and have more children. Many more young people are now moving to the towns after leaving school, so the adult population left in the village is getting smaller every year.

*◄ Horto has no rush-hour traffic, or industrial pollution, as São Paulo does. But the village relies on the visits of pilgrims every year for its survival.*

farmland separates the two communities. Any development of the village is along the edge of the tarmac road leading to the square and church. This is the route used by traffic, with small shops where visitors can stop to buy food or souvenirs. The village seems content to remain as it is for now, and those who stay will certainly enjoy cleaner air and a more relaxed lifestyle than people in São Paulo.

*Children relaxing on a Sunday afternoon in Horto.* ▼

# Glossary

**carnival** A festival held just before Lent in Brazil, where there is public entertainment and street processions.

**colonial** Where one country, the colony, is governed by people who have come from another country.

**environment** The surroundings, both natural and artificial.

**exports** Goods produced by one country and sold to other countries.

*favelas* Poor housing built of simple materials, usually found on the outskirts of cities.

*ganzá* A musical instrument consisting of a little metal box containing pebbles, used in north-east Brazil.

**hydroelectricity** Electricity made by the power of water flowing through a special generator in a dam.

**immigrants** People who move to another country to live.

**imports** Goods bought by one country from other countries.

**insurance** An arrangement that provides money in the event of losing something or becoming ill.

**irrigation** Most usually it is the use of water to help plants to grow.

**literacy** Ability to read and write.

**manioc** A plant with large, thick roots that is grown in parts of Brazil. The roots are grated to make a coarse flour that has to be pressed free of liquid and then dried.

**merchant ships** Ships used for carrying cargo.

**metro** An underground railway. The name is short for 'Metropolitan Railway'.

**migration** The movement from one part of a country to another to live.

**missionaries** People who work overseas for a church.

**palm thatch** A roof covering on the leaves of palm trees.

**pilgrims** People who travel long distances to religious centres.

**pioneers** People who prepare the way for others.

**plantations** A planted area, usually covered by the same kind of plant.

**pollution** Damage caused by a substance or condition.

**rain forest** A rich forest where over 2 metres of rain fall each year.

**republic** A type of government without a king or queen, usually ruled by an elected president.

**tributaries** Rivers or streams that flow into a larger one.

**Tropic of Capricorn** An imaginary circle around the world south of the equator where, at certain times each year, the sun appears directly overhead at noon.

# Further information

## Books to read

*Discovering Brazil* by Marion Morrison (Zoe Books, 1996)

*Country Fact Files: Brazil* by Marion Morrison (Simon & Schuster, 1993)

*Top Secret Guide to Brazil* by Marion Morrison (Highlights, 1996)

*Brazil* by Evelyn Bender (Chelsea House, 1990)

*Economically Developing Countries: Brazil* by Anna Lewington and Edward Parker (Wayland, 1995)

*The Amazon Rainforest and its People* by Marion Morrison (Wayland, 1993)

## Useful addresses

Hispanic and Luso-Brazilian Council, Canning House, 2 Belgrave Square, London SW1X 8PJ

Brazilian Embassy, 32 Green Street, London W1Y 4AT

Brazilian Contemporary Arts (BCA), Palingswicke House, 241 King Street, London W6

Brazil Network, PO Box 1325, London SW9 6BG

PICTURE ACKNOWLEDGEMENTS

All photographs except the cover are by Tony Morrison, of South American Pictures.

Cover photograph by Sue Cunningham Photographic.

All map artwork is by Peter Bull.

SOURCES

The statistics in this book are from the following sources:

*Instituto Brasileiro de Geografia e Estatistica; Anuário Estatístico do Estado de São Paulo 1993; Prefeitura Municipal de Juazeiro do Norte Europa 1995;*
United Nations: *State of the World's Population* 1995.

# Index

Page numbers in **bold** refer to photographs.